GREY MATTER

WHY IT'S GOOD TO BE OLD!

Andrews McMeel
Publishing, LLC

Kansas City

GREY MATTER

WHY IT'S GOOD TO BE OLD!

Bob Elsdale and Vasilisa

'Old' isn't old any more. There's a new kind of 'old' … and a new kind of oldie.

Take the Rolling Stones. When 'The Greatest Rock 'n' roll Band in the World' can totter onto the stage in their mid 60s and belt out 'I can't get no satisfaction', for the gazillionth time, then something quite remarkable has happened to the world.

It's not that long ago anyone over 50 would have been expected to sing 'I can't give no satisfaction'. Or, more likely, 'I'm not actually interested in satisfaction, thank you very much, I've got to have a lie down'.

Yes, sir. The Waterloo sun set very quickly on anything resembling fun in those dreary days and once it had gone everything after that was strictly a walk on the mild side. Lazy Sunday came early and once you reached two score years and ten you were in Blandland.

And after that the merest hint, the slightest suggestion, that you were even *thinking* about doing the pelvic boogie in front of 10,000 screaming kids all young enough to be your grandchildren would have been sufficient to have you lashed to a Zimmer Frame and pushed out to sea.

You weren't expected to be a groover. Correction. You weren't *allowed* to be a groover. Today's haemorrhoid hippies were simply unheard of. 'Old' was old, and it started young … but not any more. If that was the age of Niagara, this is the age of Viagra.

There's a new kid on the block – the young oldie, or 'yoldie'. If you're a yoldie you'll know the symptoms, and you won't be planning on growing old gracefully. You want some twinkle with your wrinkle. You want some rage with your age. You want to be bopping *when* you're dropping.

You want some geriantics!

If you see 60 as a celebration rather than an obligation, then this little volume is for you. Laugh at the slightly creaky joints – maybe because of the slightly creaky joints – even if it does make it hard to keep the teeth in and causes chaos with the waterworks. It's the no-Botox way to happiness.

And laughing is what it's all about. **Grey matter matters – it's good to be old.**

☞ IT'S THE GREY MATT

ER THAT MATTERS...

☞ SO KEEP A TWINKLE

IN YOUR WRINKLE...

AFTER ALL,
YOU'RE STILL ON
THE BALL.

IT'S A TIME
IN YOUR LIFE TO

CELEBRATE...

AS THEY SAY,

'LIFE'S A BEACH'...

AND THERE'S PLENTY OF TIME TO GET BOARD.

AND BE

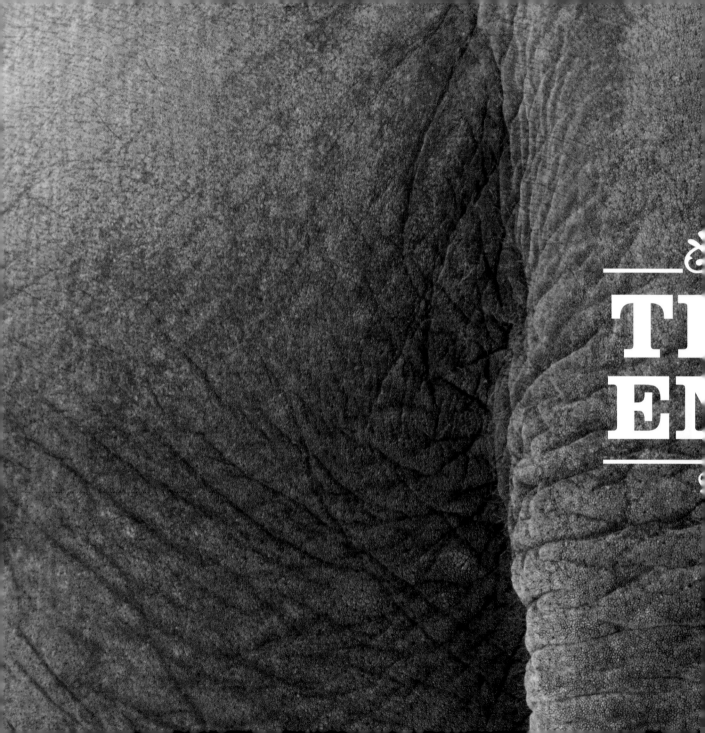

*NO ELEPHANTS WERE HARMED IN THE MAKING OF THIS BOOK.

The first time I photographed an elephant was in a car studio for an assignment. The advertising agency had visualised an elephant being beamed up by a flying saucer, the usual kind of thing agencies do. Knowing my passion for creating the unexpected, the art director suggested I shoot it. This started me thinking that we could do more with elephants.

I've managed to capture the elephants in **Grey Matter** in extraordinary positions and for that I have to give a huge amount of credit to the trainers who spend countless hours talking and working with them. It is so obvious that the elephants love their trainers and enjoy the whole experience; they will do anything for them and they do it with pleasure.

My assistant Vasilisa and I had worked out a long list of required positions for the elephants in advance for this book – the trainers were very helpful in answering our numerous questions beforehand. However, the body language of the elephants during the photography often suggested a new scenario to us. We photographed on and off for about eight months to capture the images.

The stunning beach scenes were shot on Saunton Sands in North Devon, UK. Getting the lighting right when shooting in such a location is an exercise in patience, I've lost count of the number of times we've been back to Saunton Sands …

Elephants are such wonderful, expressive, gentle and intelligent creatures, far more intelligent than any of us can possibly imagine, which is why I try to anthropomorphise them in my photographs. I consider it a privilege to work with certain animals and elephants are definitely one of them.

Bob Elsdale

Copyright ©Bob Elsdale 2006 www.bobelsdale.com

Book concept, photography and digital art Bob Elsdale and Vasilisa

This edition published in 2006 by Andrews McMeel Publishing, LLC, an Andrews McMeel Universal company, 4520 Main Street, Kansas City, Missouri 64111. No part of this publication may be reproduced (except brief extracts for the purposes of review), stored in a retrieval system or transmitted in any form by any means, electronic, mechanical, photocopying, recording or otherwise, without the prior written permission of the publisher.

First edition published in 2006 by PQ Blackwell Limited.

Text concepts by PQ Blackwell and Jim Hopkins

Artwork design by Cameron Gibb and Carolyn Lewis

Printed by Midas Printing International Limited, China

ISBN-13: 978-0-7407-6252-9
ISBN-10: 0-7407-6252-4
Library of Congress Control Number: On file

www.andrewsmcmeel.com

ACKNOWLEDGEMENTS

I would like to thank the following people and elephants for making this book possible:

Vasilisa, my assistant, for her great vision and eagle eye for detail, for her childish mind which rivals mine at times, and for her complete dedication to the job;

Gary, Kari, Joanne and all the elephants at Have Trunk Will Travel, Inc. for their help and enthusiasm throughout;

Chris Elsdale for her supreme organisational skills;

Sam Kweskin and Curtis McElhinneey, two of Los Angeles' finest photographic assistants.

Highly qualified trainers supervised the welfare of the elephants throughout the photography required for the making of this book. The owners of the elephants, Gary and Kari Johnson, are committed alongside the International Elephant Foundation to the preservation and protection of all elephants worldwide.